# FROM ~~STRESSED~~ TO **BLESSED**
## a personal journey

Frances Bradley Robinson

Copyright © 2017 by LaunchCrate Publishing &
Frances Bradley Robinson

All rights reserved. No part of this publication may be reproduced, distributed, or transmitted in any form or by any means, including photocopying, recording, or other electronic or mechanical methods, without the prior written permission of the publisher, except in the case of brief quotations embodied in critical reviews and certain other noncommercial uses permitted by copyright law. For permission requests, email the publisher with subject "Attention: Permissions Coordinator," at the address below.

LaunchCrate Publishing
info@launchcrate.com
www.launchcrate.com

*Ordering Information:*
Quantity sales. Special discounts are available on quantity purchases by corporations, associations, and others. For details, contact the publisher at the email address above. Orders by U.S. trade bookstores and wholesalers.

Library of Congress Control Number: 2017957745

ISBN 978-1-947506-00-8 (paperback)

Printed in the United States of America
10 9 8 7 6 5 4 3 2 1

First Edition

Cover Design: C. L. Fails

Dedicated to my favorite daughter,
Stacey Beatrice Robinson Knoell.

# Preface

Have you ever felt stressed? Silly question! Of course you have felt stressed. I am sure that there is probably not a day that has gone by, when you have not experienced some degree of stress. Perhaps you overslept, or you misplaced your keys. Or maybe you were stuck in traffic.

Stress appears in a variety of forms and lasts varying lengths of time. So imagine how it would feel if, in addition to the usual inconveniences that you encounter on a daily basis, you also experienced even greater stress that severely impacted your lifestyle. What if you lost a loved one, or you were diagnosed with a life threatening illness, or you struggled through an aggressive medical treatment, or you moved to a new residence, or you underwent a radical surgical procedure, or you sold a home? Perhaps you have already faced one or more of those challenges. But what if you experienced all of them within a relatively short period of time? While any one of the aforementioned situations can stand alone as a major source of stress, I experienced all of them within a period of just eighteen months.

Now, allow me hasten to acknowledge that while I have not been totally without stress during any other period of time in my life, I am also keenly aware of the fact that I am not the only person in the world who has faced a series of life altering challenges within a short period of time. However, when my daughter asked me to write about my experience with a serious medical condition for a local health club newsletter, I was

## PREFACE

not prepared to do so at that time. I simply had not yet organized my thoughts. Yet when I did begin to write, I felt compelled to include the series of events that I describe in this narrative, as inspiration for my chosen theme, 'from stressed to blessed'. Consequently, with further encouragement from other relatives and friends who were eye witnesses to my journey, I decided to write this memoir as an expression of my faith. It is a testimony of a faith that will hopefully inspire at least one person to find a blessing in any situation.

# Eighteen Months

*June 9, 2013 to November 26, 2014*

- I. THE LOSS
- II. THE DIAGNOSIS
- III. THE TREATMENT
- IV. THE MOVE
- V. THE SURGERY
- VI. THE SALE

# The Loss

I will never forget the Sunday morning of June 9, 2013 when I awoke to discover that my husband, of forty-four years, had died in his sleep. I could not believe that this could happen. In spite of the fact that doctors had referred him to palliative care nearly three years before, the shock of his death was devastating.

As relatives and friends gathered in my home on that day to comfort me, I was numb. I found it very difficult to make sense of my new reality.

During the days that followed, amidst the turmoil of making funeral arrangements, I grieved through a multitude of emotions. First of all, I wanted to deny that it ever happened. While feeling depressed, I also felt a little angry. After all, I had tried desperately to make sure that his quality of life was as good as it could possibly be. And as his primary care giver, I had spent countless days in hospital emergency rooms with him.

My questions were many. Why did this have to happen? Why couldn't my husband have simply given up smoking or drinking? Could the horror of being on the ground in tanks during his service in the Vietnam War, back in the nineteen sixties, have caused him to actually have a death wish? An awful thought, I must admit. But it did, none the less, cause me to fail to understand why he had seemed to refuse to heed the advice of doctors, or anyone else who tried to help him, in any effort to save his own life. I felt guilty, too, because I

## *The Loss*

was unable to help him more. What more could I have done? Where do I go from here? I was at a total loss. And as I struggled to cope with my own private pity party, I felt both physically and mentally drained. I was exhausted. Yes, I was stressed.

As time has passed, I have, however on a daily basis, struggled very hard to simply accept the fact that because I will never be able to change what happened in the past, that it is in my best interest to at least cherish the good memories that I do have, and to embrace the present, which is now my new reality. I now constantly remind myself of the fact that I had, indeed, been fortunate enough to have been married to my junior high school sweetheart, a wonderful man, for many pleasant years. And for that reason, I am grateful.

Yes, I am blessed.

# The Diagnosis

Fast-forward five months to November 19, 2013. I had not felt very well for quite some time, mostly because I was consumed by mental, as well as, physical exhaustion and just overall stress. Upon discovering a lump in my left breast, I decided to get a long overdue medical checkup. My mammogram report revealed that the lump was the size of a marble and required further testing. During a series of doctor visits, I had a sonogram, a CT scan, a MRI, a bone scan, as well as an eco-cardiogram, to name a few. And with each additional test, the prognosis was dismal, confirming a most unwelcome result.

'You have breast cancer.' Something that I never dreamed that I would ever hear, and yet those were her exact words. After all, I was still mourning the death of my husband. How could I possibly cope with another crisis so soon?

Now because, I had always considered myself to be a rather super private person, I did not want to burden anyone with this new revelation, not even my only daughter, who had just months before, lost her father. You see I believed that, as the product of a generation of parents who appeared to consider discussion of certain matters, such as a serious illness, or infidelity, or adoption, to be prohibited, that I should just keep my diagnosis to myself. And unlike my impression of the younger generation that seems to post just about everything on social media, I also felt a close kinship, that I perceived of my own generation, to reluctantly reveal information that was just too personal.

So as a result of such limiting thoughts, I kept all of those previous tests and diagnostic procedures to myself. And because I was not aware of anyone, in the whole wide world, in whom I could confide, I suffered in silence. Furthermore, as a church musician who had played for many funerals of persons whom I later discovered had succumbed to cancer, I also associated the 'c' word with death. Therefore, when the hospital physician called to confirm my diagnosis, I immediately decided that the end was near for me, and that I did not want anyone to know. I was again devastated. I was depressed. I felt hopeless.

I received that infamous call on the Friday before Thanksgiving, just hours before I was scheduled to travel from Kansas City, KS to Branson, MO with three friends who planned to engage in a marathon card playing adventure. During the four-hour drive to our destination, in addition to 'solving the problems of the world' through casual conversation, we also listened to an audio book. While I am sure that the story was very interesting to the other passengers, I could not avoid focusing on the part of the plot that described a mother who was dying of breast cancer. As I listened to the tape, I felt empty and struggled to find joy in anything that happened during the trip.

When I did eventually confide in one of the friends, and revealed to her the real reason for my apparent lack of enthusiasm, she advised me to seek a second opinion.

So, within an hour upon our return to Kansas City from Branson, I changed from one car to another, as I joined my daughter, her husband and my two grandchildren on a road trip to Arlington, NE. While I very much looked forward to celebrating the holidays with my daughter and her in-laws on my first Thanksgiving without my husband, I also

## *The Diagnosis*

felt an urgency to tell her about my diagnosis as soon as possible. It was during a drive to Target in Elcorn, NE on Black Friday, that I did share the news. She whole heartily endorsed the decision to seek a second opinion. We then, together scheduled several appointments with, not only the original doctor and surgeon, but also with a new staff of professionals.

The second opinion did, indeed, confirm the first. Yes. I had breast cancer. But for some strange reason those words from the new team of doctors did not resonate quite as harshly with me, as they did when I heard them for the first time only days before. Instead of scheduling an immediate mastectomy, followed by chemotherapy and possibly radiation treatments with a projected success rate of a little over sixty percent that the first team of doctors proposed, the new staff of professionals were much more optimistic, as they prescribed a procedure that was a total reverse of the aforementioned schedule. They began by explaining their confidence in a recently approved treatment for my type of cancer, that had proven to yield a nearly one hundred percent rate for cure. That was great news! Their plan of action involved the application of chemotherapy first, with the goal of reducing the spread of any cancer cells, to later be followed by an inevitable mastectomy, and a possible series of radiation treatments.

To my relief, as well as to the relief of my family, the doctors also confirmed that, for my type of cancer, there was no need to pursue genetic testing. That was great news!

Yes, I am blessed.

# The Treatment

On Sunday, December 29, 2013, following the confirmation of my diagnosis of breast cancer, I shared the news with a handful of friends at church. And because my first treatment was scheduled for the next day, I felt compelled to inform the wife of my Pastor about the reason for which I could not attend a scheduled meeting. She then asked if I would mind if she shared my situation with the Pastor. I thought that perhaps it would be appropriate under the circumstances. When the Pastor approached me, while I was sitting at the piano in preparation for the morning service, and asked if I would mind if he informed the congregation of my situation, my initial reaction was an absolute 'Yes', I would mind. After all, I was, indeed a private person, and I was not ready to share such personal information with the entire world. I must admit that keeping such a huge secret to myself was very draining. Yet, because I was unaware of any close friends who had gone through what I was about to face, I did not want to burden anyone with my problem. After all, who would care? Everybody has enough problems of their own.

The Pastor insisted, however, in convincing me to understand that he believed prayer could have a powerful impact on my imminent journey. I then, reluctantly consented to his request, and when he waited until the end of the service to inform the congregation of my situation, the shock was quite apparent throughout the sanctuary. I now must admit that his announcement triggered a pivotal point in my life. As one person after another approached me, following the service, I felt as if the weight of the world had suddenly been lifted off my shoulders.

To my amazement, people seemed to come out of the woodwork, to share inspiring survival stories about their personal journey with cancer, or their association with relatives or friends who had conquered the disease. In many cases their connection to the disease was not common knowledge, and yet they were willing to confide in me, in an effort to somehow relieve my apprehension. If only I had been aware of their stories sooner, I might not have suffered in silence for so long,. And it is for that reason, that I now realize the importance of sharing personal struggles with others, not for fear of ridicule or a plea for sympathy, but when appropriate, for the possibility of actually helping someone who may be dealing with similar issues. I, therefore, having heard many positive stories, am very grateful for the friends, and sometimes strangers, who became, a much appreciated source of support, and helped me to cope with the depth of my situation.

And now for the technical talk. The pathology report, that I received at the conclusion of my treatments, documents that my diagnosis was confirmed on December 18, 2013. The official name for my condition was 'invasive ductal carcinoma of the breast'. Quite a mouthful, I must admit. Yet, I learned that the term simply refers to a tumor that starts in the milk duct and spreads to other parts of the body through the blood or lymphatic system. The size of my tumor, roughly 5 cm (picture a AA battery), was a fast growing Grade 3. My hormone receptor status, HER-2, described fast growing cancerous breast tissue cells that overproduced the HER-2 gene, which in turn, produced extra protein receptors on the cell surface, and ultimately triggered the cells to divide and to multiply at an accelerated rate, thus contributing to the rapid growth of the tumor. And because my results were positive on a specific test of the breast tissue called IHC (ImmunoHistoChemistry) that measures the protein made by the HER-2 gene, I underwent intravenous treatment of an anti-HER-2 antibody therapy called trastuzumab (Herceptin) designed to prevent further growth of the tumor by interrupting the growth signal and slowing the progression of the disease.

So, for a total of fifty-seven weeks, beginning on December 30, 2013, I reported to the University of Kansas Hospital Cancer Center / Medical Oncology Unit for chemotherapy treatments at three week intervals. My first treatment of taxotere, perjeta, and herceptin were administered through a vein in my hand. The after affect of that method of treatment, however, proved to be extremely uncomfortable, resulting in a chemical rash on my forearm and hand, that lasted about two weeks. Most treatments, thereafter, however, were administered through a Porta-cath that was inserted near my right shoulder. Thank goodness, those treatments proved to be much more humane. Although a day of treatments initially lasted about eight hours, the length of time gradually decreased with each appointment. I am, indeed, very grateful for many relatives and friends who actually voluntarily accompanied me to many of my appointments.

I completed the taxotere and perjeta injections on April 16, 2014, after just fifteen weeks. I frequently referred to that aggressive combination of chemicals as 'industrial strength' because the side effects were intense. And while the purpose of the perjeta was to reduce the growth of additional cancer cells, the purpose of the taxotere was to drastically reduce my white blood cell count, the side effects of which caused me to lose my hair, my nails, and my appetite.

I remember brushing my hair after the initial treatment when to my amazement, a handful of hair appeared in my brush. In the days that followed, I lost batches of hair and was soon completely bald. While most of my nails simply chipped frequently because they were so fragile, some actually came off. I also completely lost my appetite. What? - turning down a slice of pizza because it made me nauseous, or having no desire for a doughnut because it gave me diarrhea? It was unreal! My taste buds were shot. As a result, I lost nearly sixty pounds very rapidly during the time that I was on the infamous 'industrial strength' medications. I might add here, that shortly after my husband's death, I recall having looked in the mirror and having declared that I really needed to lose weight. In hindsight, however, I think that perhaps I should have been a bit more specific on just how I planned to accomplish that goal. I was not prepared to do it in such a drastic way.

Now, allow me to describe a significant, yet totally unexpected event that occurred while I was still undergoing chemotherapy treatments.

## *From Blessed to Stressed*

It was Wednesday, February 26, 2014, when I actually felt my weakest, both physically and mentally. It was also my seventieth birthday, and yet I could barely get out of bed. Several people called or sent birthday messages, and I even had one visitor. But for the majority of the day, I felt simply lousy and quite physically challenged, mostly due to extreme nausea and diarrhea. So when the church choir director called to find out why I was not at rehearsal an hour earlier than the regularly scheduled time, I admitted to him that I was not aware of a time change, and therefore, promised to get to the church as soon as I could. After all, it had been my goal to not only make my bed each morning, but to go somewhere, anywhere, every single day, whether I felt like it or not, (my motto: 'mind over matter'), and that day would be no exception.

Upon my arrival at the church, in my haste to enter the sanctuary, I barely noticed that the parking lot was nearly full. I thought briefly,

*The Treatment*

however, that some meeting was being held, perhaps in the basement of the church, that would not interfere with the rehearsal. As the parking lot attendant directed me to park near the entrance of the church and walked with me to the door, he uncharacteristically escorted me inside the sanctuary, where a crowd of people greeted me with, "Surprise!".

To my total amazement, the sanctuary was full of well over a hundred relatives and friends who were there to be part of a surprise birthday celebration for me, for which absolutely no one, I repeat, no one, not even my precious daughter, had given me even the slightest hint. The event, a genuinely total surprise to me, consisted of an outstanding program with many prayers, lots of inspirational music, several tributes, and a beautiful reception in the basement of the church at the conclusion of the 'service'.

When I was called upon to give remarks, I

remember being in a total daze and I do not even recall if the idea of a birthday celebration ever crossed my mind while I was speaking. I do remember thinking, however, that I had only one long awaited message to deliver to the world, and that message was 'the importance of early detection' as it relates to cancer. I vaguely recall rambling about yearly checkups and the like. Needless-to-say, I was totally overwhelmed, humbled, and yet eternally grateful for the outpouring of love that I felt. And as I left the church, I felt that the power of so many prayers, compelled me to embrace my faith even more, and encouraged me to develop a stronger desire to seek God's help in conquering the disease.

I felt so well, as a matter of fact, that I even scheduled a trip, for the following month to Las Vegas, NV, to participate in a national bridge tournament. After all, playing duplicate bridge has always been one of my favorite pastimes. And although I had warning signs to perhaps

## THE TREATMENT

postpone that trip, I ignored them and thought, 'no problem', I will be all right. What was I thinking?

As I stated before, one of the side effects, of my chemotherapy treatments, was a lack of appetite. So during the trip, because I could barely eat, I had very little energy. I recall ordering food, then, not being able to eat very much of it. I, on several occasions, paid for a friend's meal, just so she could share with me, maybe only one or two bites. I literally had to force myself to eat even that. I soon became so self conscious of eating with a group, that I often chose to eat alone in the fast food court of the hotel. On one occasion, when it was obvious that I was not going to finish my meal, a rather disheveled man approached my table to ask if he could have my leftovers. Without hesitation, I gave them to him, because I did not want to just throw unused food away. From then on, whenever I ate in that same area, I felt comfortable when I shared my leftovers with complete strangers. With just a couple of bites, ever so often, I managed to have enough energy to at least take a few more steps. How I was able to play intelligible bridge during that time is extremely questionable, but, I imagine that because I was such a pitiful sight, my partner just never bothered to complain.

Now back to the treatments. While I continued to receive herceptin for the entire fifty seven weeks, my hair began to grow back shortly after I completed the 'industrial strength' medications. My nails, also, grew. However, I also continued to receive neulasta shots, the after effects of which were severe bone pain throughout my entire body. The pain was so intense, that I could often barely walk and would frequently lose my balance and even fall, resulting in visits to a couple of hospital emergency rooms with facial bruises. It was only upon the casual recommendation by a hospital nurse, however, that taking Claritin two days before each neulasta treatment might cause the pain to be less intense, that I gave it a try. Not all of the pain was relieved, but it was, at least, no longer debilitating. Imagine, Claritin, designed to relieve symptoms of allergies, could actually help to reduce pain. It was a surprise to me, but it seemed to work.

My last chemotherapy treatment was on February 3, 2015. Hallelujah! Subsequent follow up appointments with my medical oncologist were scheduled for every three to six months for the first two years. At the writing of the memoir, I must now see my specialist every six to twelve months for the next three years. So for now, I am 'cancer free'! And that is great news! Yes, again!

I am blessed!

# The Move

On March 14, 2014, just under three months after my first chemotherapy treatment, having been on a waiting list since the date of that first treatment, I moved out of my house, of twenty-five plus years, into an apartment close to my daughter and her family. You see, years prior to this move, my daughter had begged my husband and me to move out of our house that was not in the best condition, and was apparently not becoming any easier to maintain. We, especially my husband, had no intention of moving at that time. Fast forward to the death of my husband, when my daughter pleaded with me to move out of the house. I, again, did not feel an urgency to do so. It was not until I began the chemotherapy treatments, that I reluctantly consented to move.

Now, had I been a bit younger, perhaps in my sixties, I might have considered moving into a large space. But at age seventy, all I really wanted was a one bedroom bungalow, with the option to relocate quickly, if necessary. My daughter, however, convinced me to at least consider a two bedroom apartment. We did, indeed, find one that was close to my daughter. Instead of driving nearly forty-five miles round trip every day, we are within three miles, of each other. The apartment was, obviously much smaller than the house, which meant that the need to downsize presented it's own unique set of challenges. To say that there was some degree of stress, associated with deciding which items to pack from the old house, what to purchase for the new apartment, and of course, the ultimate task of how to unpack it all,

## THE MOVE

would be an understatement for even a person in the best of health. I am, however again, eternally grateful for relatives and friends, who pitched in, and helped to make the move much easier.

While I have never been a slave to fashion, especially in the area of home decor, I did spend many, many hours, prior to the move, simply gazing at home decorating magazines, in an effort to visualize how I might decorate my new apartment. I also enjoyed occasionally taking short, very short, walks through home furnishing departments of various stores, just to get a picture of what I wanted. And even though I initially must have thought that I was shopping to furnish a mansion or something of that magnitude, because my selections were so much larger than the space in which I was to live, I quickly saw the light, and managed to scale down many of my original ideas. I now, jokingly, refer to my apartment as a 'glorified dorm room' with two major themes. It consists of a 'great' room that I have divided into a living room with a musical theme, and a dining room with a card playing motif. While several of my relatives and friends actually expressed doubt about my ability to decorate my new home, hopefully because of my diminished physical stamina and not my reputation, I believe that they were quite surprised when they saw the final product. I was pleased, and felt a great sense of satisfaction when everything was put in place.

I am now grateful for a multitude of amenities that come with my new home, such as an attached garage, no steps to climb, a washer and dryer in my own unit, a spacious master bedroom and master bath, a patio that faces a lovely courtyard, access to twenty-four hour maintenance, and free use of a clubhouse that has - wait for it - a ping pong table, which my daughter claims was the main reason that I chose the location.

For the first year or so in my new apartment, I

## *The Move*

must admit that my reply to the question, "How do you like your new place?" was, "It's Okay." After all, I missed my former residence, with it's close proximity to a majority of my many personal activities. After two years, my reply was, "It's Okay. I kind of like it". It is only as I approach my third year anniversary in my new residence, that I can honestly say, "I love this place!" I now, truly, appreciate having made the decision to move. I am closer to my immediate family. I am very happy.

Yes, I am blessed!

# The Surgery

Only two months after I moved into the apartment, four months after my first chemotherapy treatment, and eleven months after the death of my husband, I underwent major surgery. On May 14, 2014, I had a bilateral mastectomy. I know this might sound strange, but there is a possibility that because I actually had not been allowed an enormous amount of time to process all of my most recent challenges, I actually looked forward to this procedure. After all that I had survived, why not at least be optimistic?

I remember waking up in the recovery room, to a room full of relatives and friends, with a smile on my face (or I, at least, felt a smile in my heart). I remember thinking, 'I am so grateful to be alive!'. The surgery proved to be the least of my concerns. As a matter of fact, during preconsultation with my surgeon, I casually requested that she schedule my surgery so that I could recover in time to defend my title as 'ping pong champion' at the annual family Fourth of July get-together. I later discovered that my request was actually written on my official medical chart.

Prior to the surgery, I consented to donate excess surgical tissue to the Biospecimen Repository at the University of Kansas Medical Center for research studies. I also chose to forego reconstructive surgery, because I simply did not feel the need to endure more physical trauma. While I spent only one night in the hospital, during the weeks that followed I patiently drained the tubes that remained after the surgery, on a daily basis. I no longer have the tubes, however, as I struggle to accept my new body image, I hasten to remind myself of how grateful I am to have survived yet another major stressful situation.

Yes, again, I am blessed!

# The Sale

It was not until early November, 2014, six months after I moved into the apartment, that I nearly panicked when I realized that I still owned a house that was unoccupied and needed to be sold. Another opportunity to be stressed? Yes. But I quickly consulted a real estate agent, who found a buyer within days after the house was listed. That was the good news. The not so good news centered around the fact that I needed to remove all items from the house prior to the sale. Hence, I was forced to quickly decide that, because a garage sale in the middle of winter was a rather impractical idea, my best option was to schedule an estate sale for those items that I had not already taken to the apartment, nor given to relatives or friends. While most estate sale agents required a minimum of six weeks to stage a home, I found an agent who was willing to fulfill my request with less than four weeks to complete the task.

The estate sale was a success, and I was out of the house by the closing date which was the Wednesday before Thanksgiving Day. The only unfortunate after affect of such a hasty move was the need to find storage space for a few additional, last minute, shall we say, sentimental items that I thought I simply could not live without. While my garage is still a bit cluttered, and I did rent a public storage unit that I will eventually resolve, there is hope. As for now, I no longer have the hassle, nor the responsibility, of maintaining a house. Hallelujah! And for that reason, again, I am blessed!

# Epilogue

Now, for the real reason that I have written this memoir. It has, been, unquestionably, therapeutic. But, most of all, it has given me, a formerly very private person, the opportunity to express my understanding of the need for people to feel comfortable about sharing their stories with one another. Everyone has a story!!! And this is mine. No person should feel alone in this journey called life.

While eighteen months is really only a 'drop in the bucket' compared to seventy years, I did experience quite a heavy dose of unusual stress during that short span of time. My husband died, I was diagnosed with breast cancer, I underwent aggressive chemotherapy treatments, I moved to an apartment, I had bilateral mastectomy, and I sold my house.

But "Through it All ... He kept me In the Midst of It All". And if the meaning of the saying "... What doesn't kill you, is suppose to make you stronger..." is actually true, then I definitely feel stronger now. I have so much to be thankful for. While tomorrow is never promised to anyone, I also realize that everything happens for a reason. Perhaps God allowed me to experience those eighteen months of extreme stress, so that by sharing my testimony through this narrative, my daughter, my two granddaughters, and others who face difficult challenges, may be able to find the strength to see hope in, and the revelation of, a blessing in any situation, just as I have done and will continue to do. The following lyrics come to

## Epilogue

mind:

> *"If I can help somebody, as I pass along.*
> *If I can cheer somebody, with a word or song.*
> *If I can show somebody, that he's traveling wrong.*
> *Then my living shall not be in vain"*

I, therefore, would like to share just a few additional insights of which I have recently become even more keenly aware. First of all, I pledge to never take the blessing of waking up each day for granted. I believe more firmly in the power of prayer. I am grateful for the prayers and the support of my family of relatives and friends, who are incidentally far, far too numerous to even attempt to list, but they know who they are, and I thank them immensely! I realize too, that a determination to set, as well as to accomplish, realistic daily goals, even when one's physical stamina is compromised, is extremely important in the recovery process. I am relieved to know that not all cancer is terminal. I am also convinced that, while early detection is so very important in the diagnosis of any physical disease, the 'elephant in the room' issue, very well may be, the recognition that, the need to receive emotional/mental help before stress threatens one's physical health, is an extremely important factor.

I now appreciate more than ever, the wisdom of two scriptures, Philippians 4:6 that reads:

> *"Don't worry about anything,*
> *Instead, pray about everything.*
> *Tell God what you need, and*
> *Thank Him for all He has done";*

and Psalm 118:24 that declares:

> *"This is the day that the Lord has made.*
> *Let us rejoice and be glad in it."*

## *Epilogue*

I am, indeed, grateful to be alive. At this stage in my life, I casually, yet seriously, often say that it definitely beats the alternative. I realize, too, that because 'you only live once', now is the time for me to celebrate, and to enjoy the life that I still have.

Hence, it is my desire that, if by chance any part of this memoir has inspired you to find hope in any stressful situation, that you, too, will declare,

"I AM BLESSED!"

# About the Author

Frances Elizabeth Bradley Robinson, the mother of one daughter (Stacey), a son-in-law (Troy), and grandmother of two girls (Alazne and Matea), is a retired music teacher. Having spent much of her life as a volunteer in a variety of civic, as well as, professional organizations, she has established a legacy of service throughout her community. She is currently a musician at her church, and in addition to playing ping pong, enjoys many card games, especially duplicate bridge.

www.ingramcontent.com/pod-product-compliance
Lightning Source LLC
Chambersburg PA
CBHW021452080526
44588CB00009B/819